I M A G E S

Tools

Karen Bryant-Mole

Heinemann

First published in Great Britain by Heinemann Publishers (Oxford) Ltd
Halley Court, Jordan Hill, Oxford OX2 8EJ

MADRID ATHENS PARIS FLORENCE PRAGUE WARSAW
PORTSMOUTH NH CHICAGO SAO PAULO SINGAPORE TOKYO
MELBOURNE AUCKLAND IBADAN GABORONE JOHANNESBURG

Designed by Jean Wheeler
Commissioned photography by Zul Mukhida
Printed in Hong Kong

00 99 98 97 96
10 9 8 7 6 5 4 3 2 1

ISBN 0 431 06289 7

British Library Cataloguing in Publication Data
Bryant-Mole, Karen
Tools. – (Images Series)
I. Title II. Series
621.9

Some of the more difficult words in this book are explained in the glossary.

Acknowledgements

The Publishers would like to thank the following for permission to reproduce photographs.Chapel Studios; 12 (right) and 21 (right) John Heinrich, 20 (both) Zul Mukhida, 13 (right) and 21 (left) Graham Horner, Zefa; 12 (left) Joan Baron, 13 (left)

Contents

In the garden

These are garden tools for children.

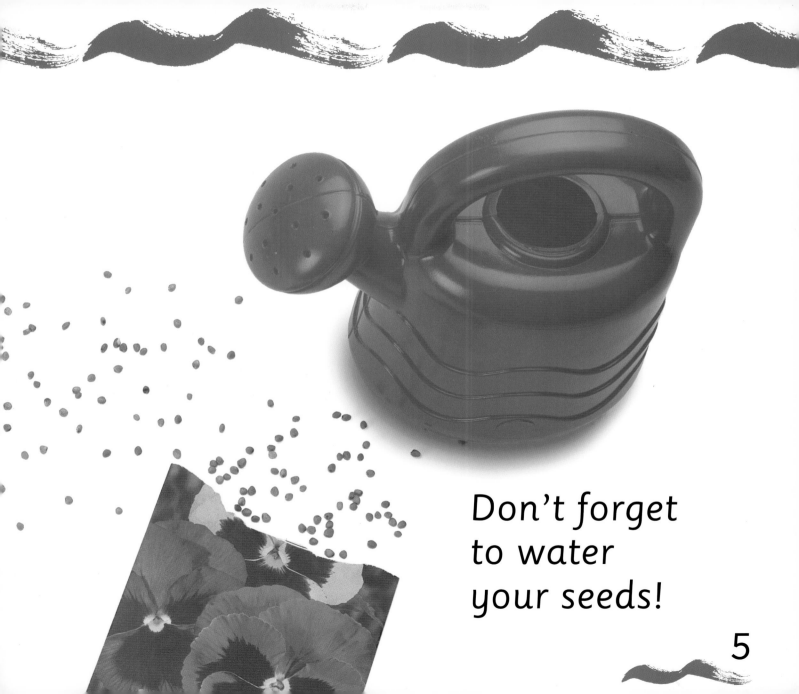

Don’t forget
to water
your seeds!

In the kitchen

pastry
cutters

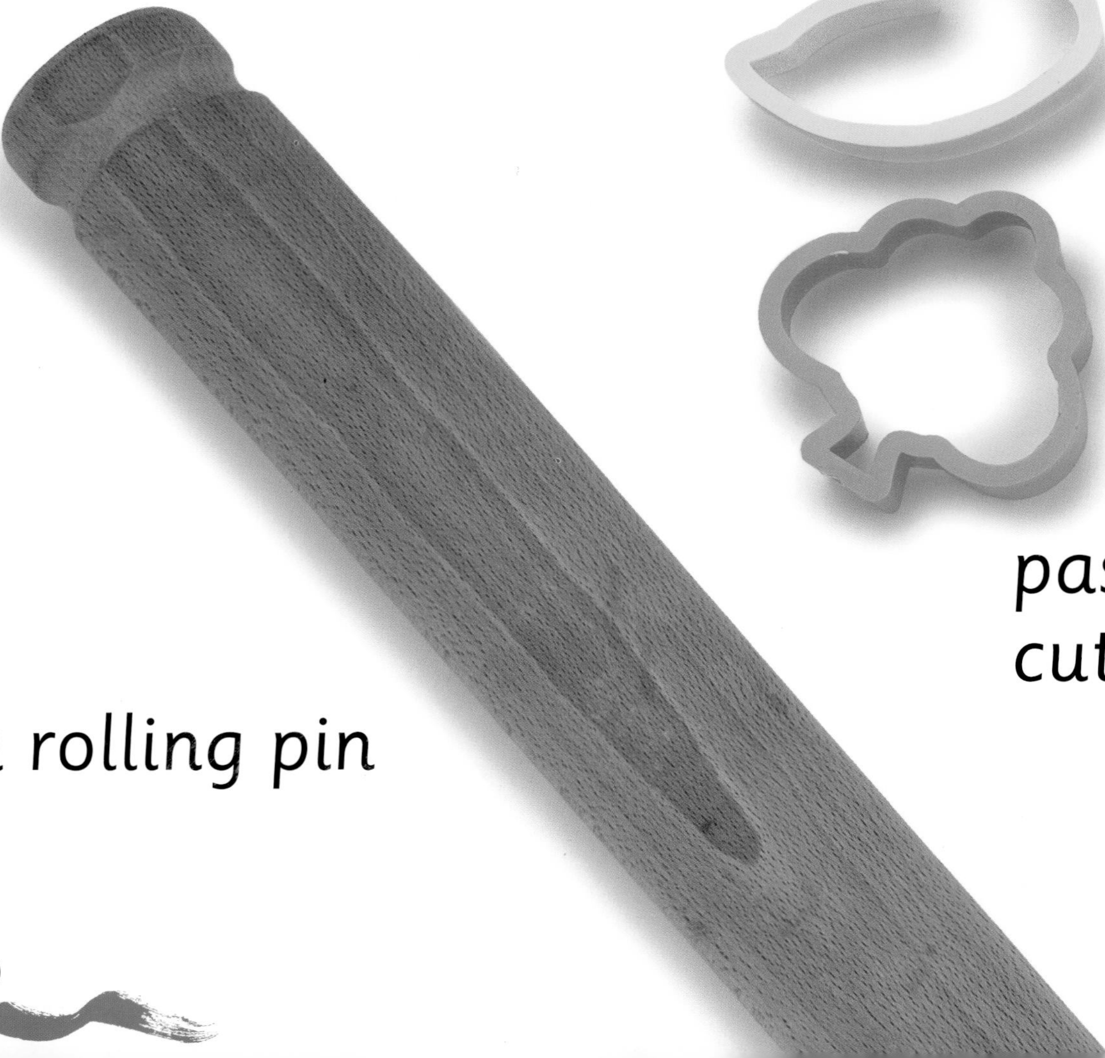

a rolling pin

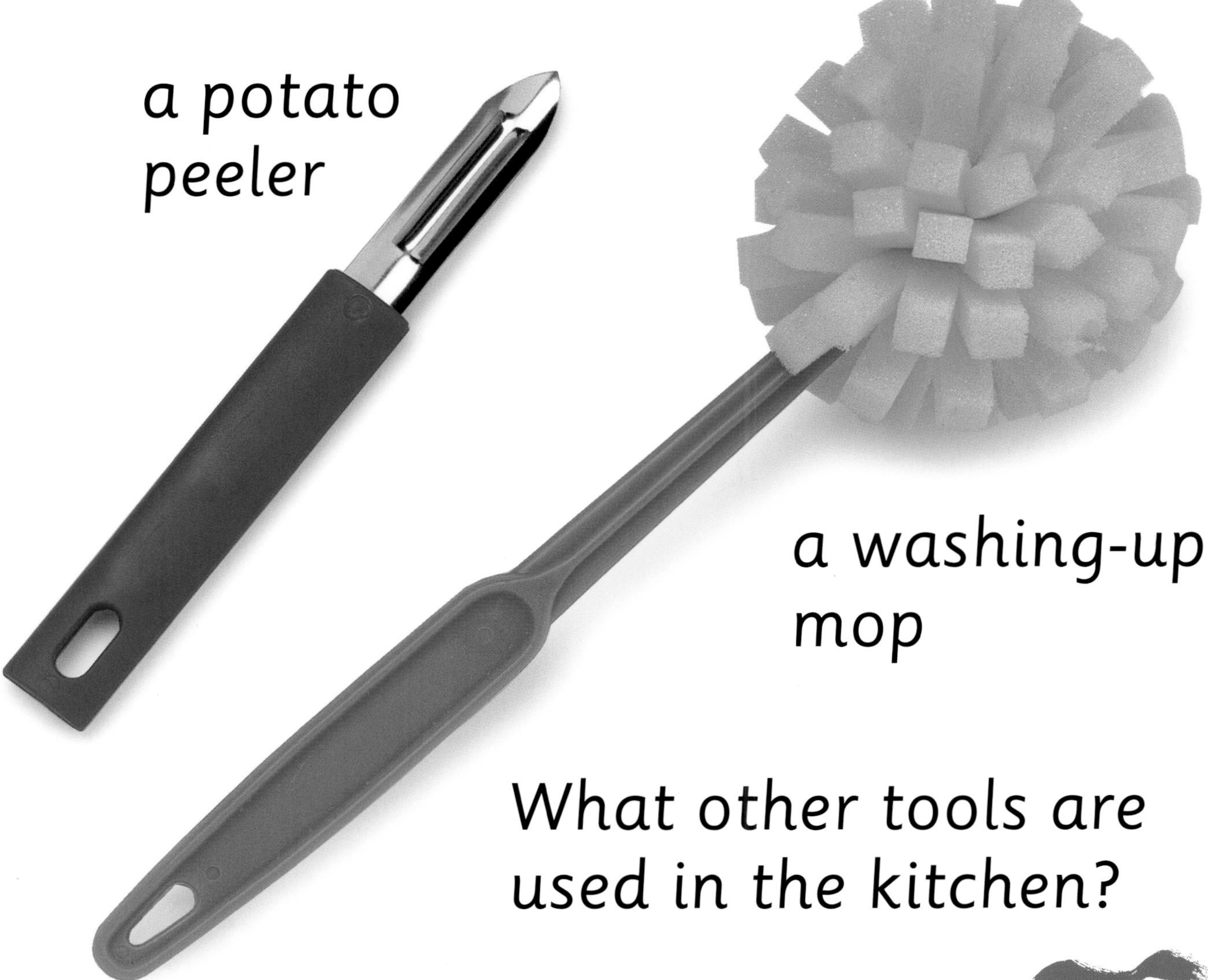

a potato
peeler

a washing-up
mop

What other tools are
used in the kitchen?

Meal-time

People can eat with
different types of cutlery.

fork
knife
spoon

At school

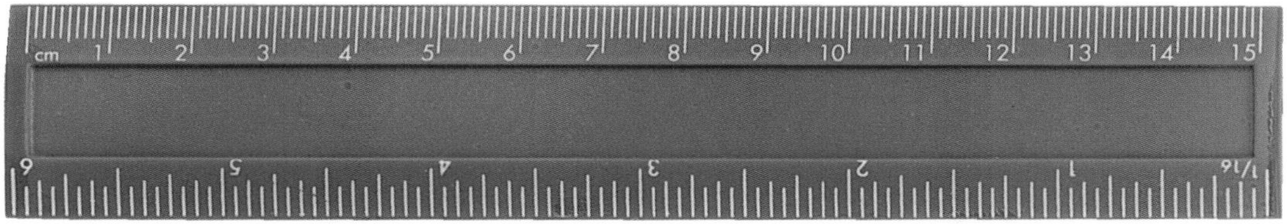

a ruler

a calculator

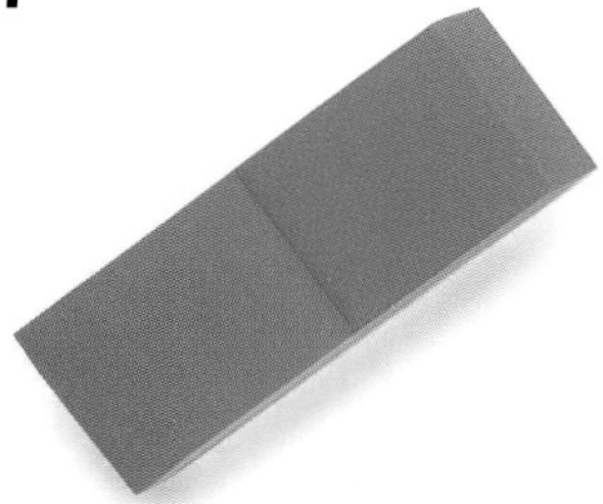

a rubber

a pen

a pencil
sharpener

pencils

Do you use
these tools at
your school?

Building sites

These builders are using lots of different tools.

This is a good place to keep tools!

Keeping clean

What tools do we use to keep ourselves clean?

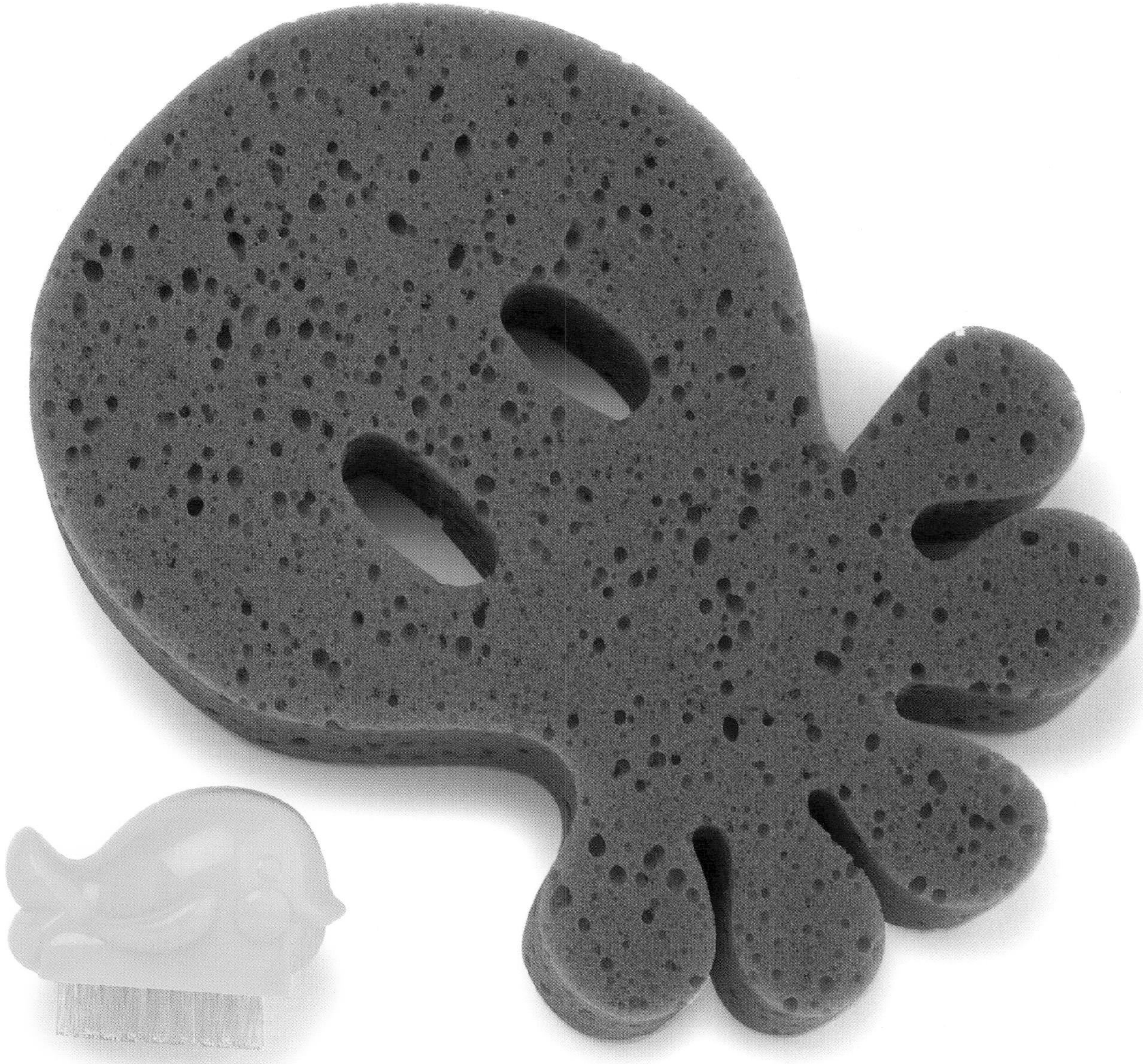

Art and craft

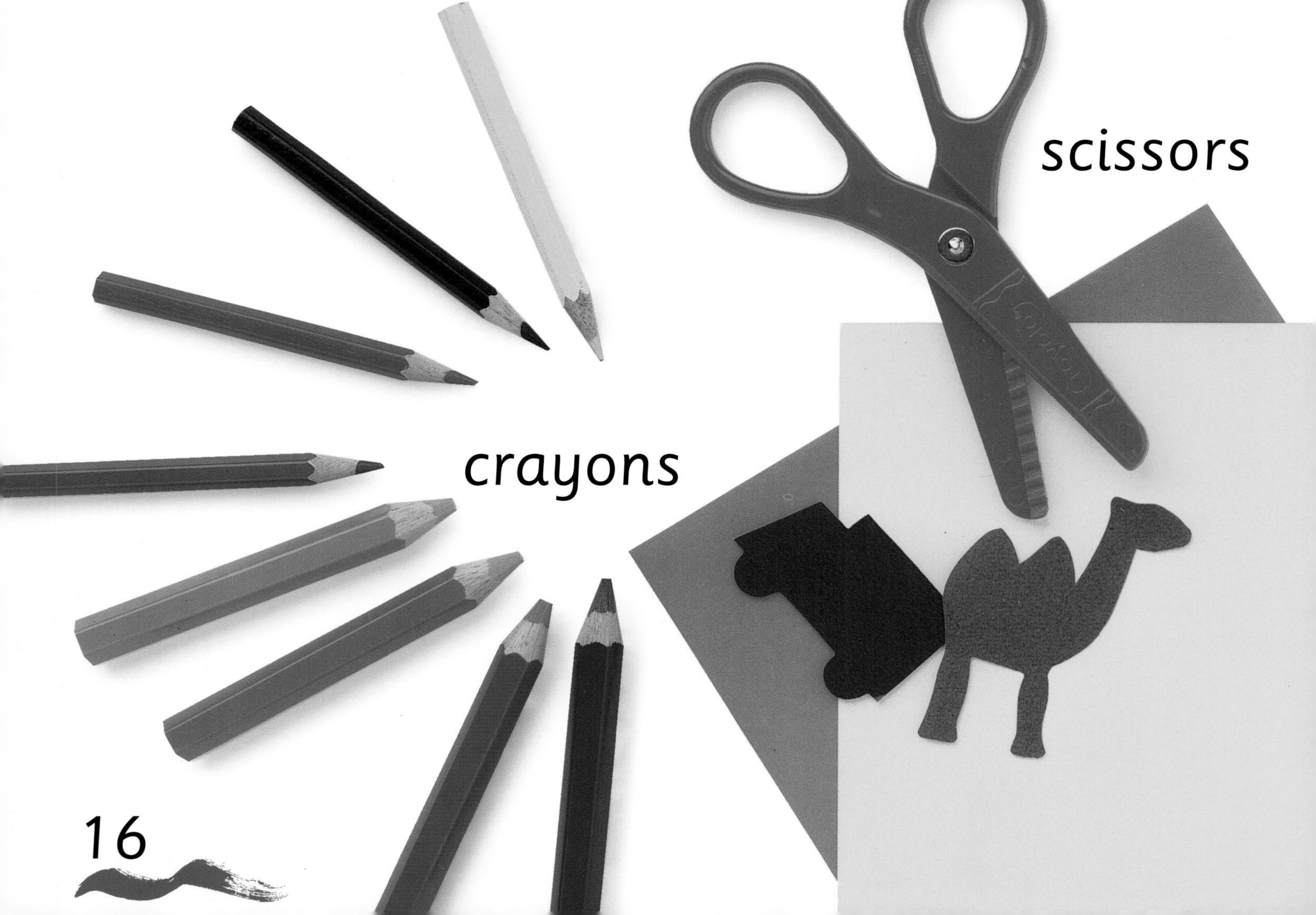

We use these tools
to make pictures
and models.

glue
stick

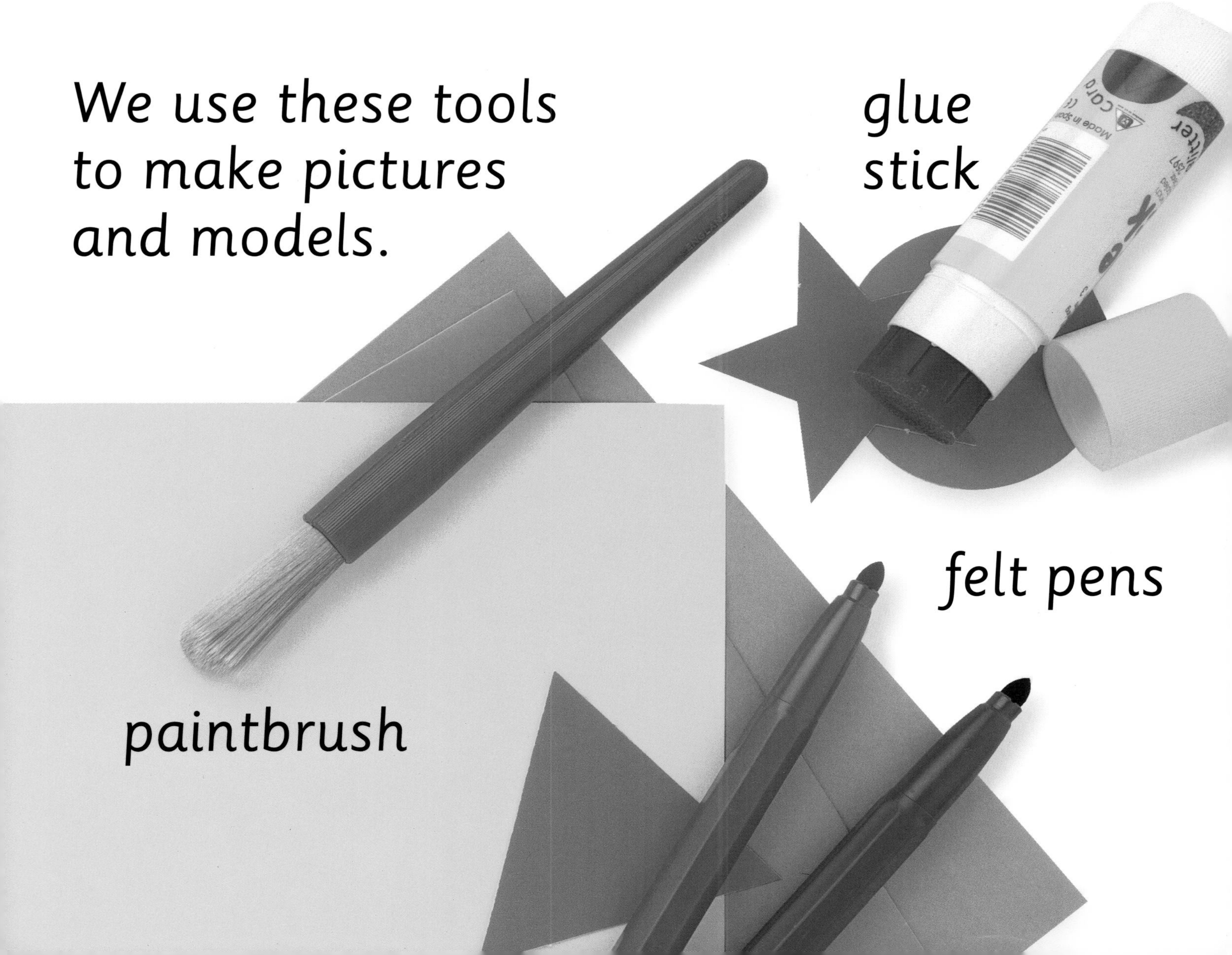

felt pens

paintbrush

Doctors' tools

This pretend doctors' set is fun to play with.

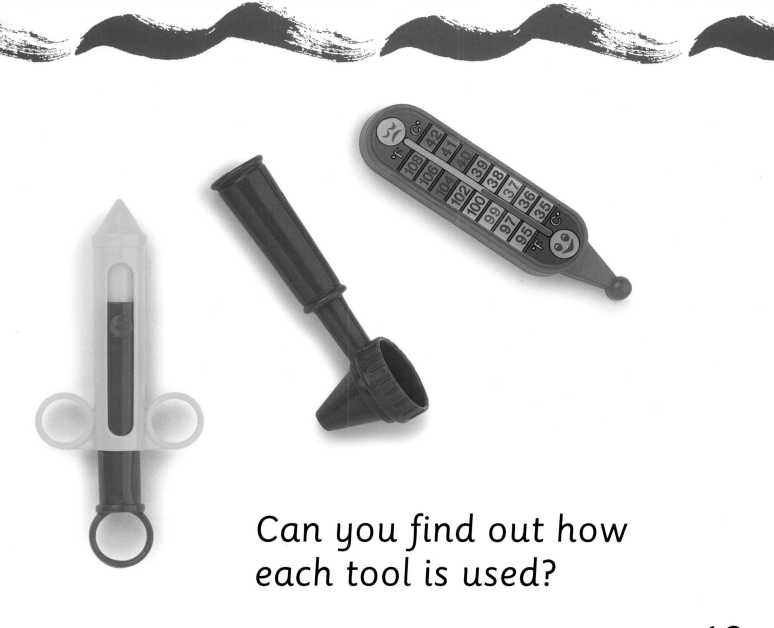

Can you find out how
each tool is used?

At work

People often use special tools in their work.

blacksmith

dentist

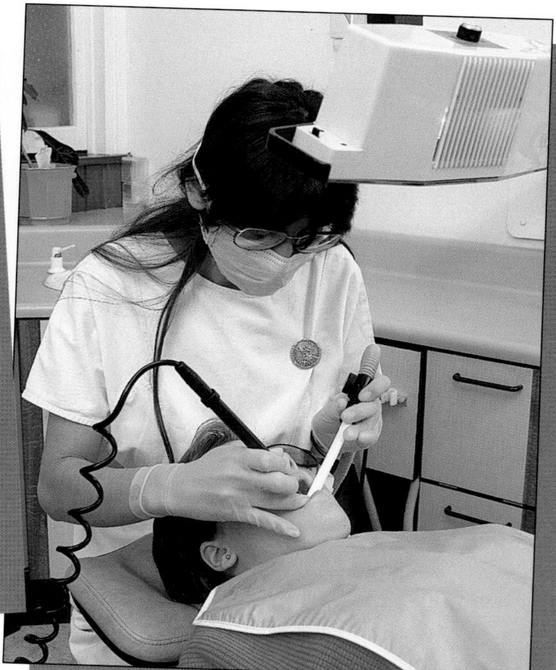

chef

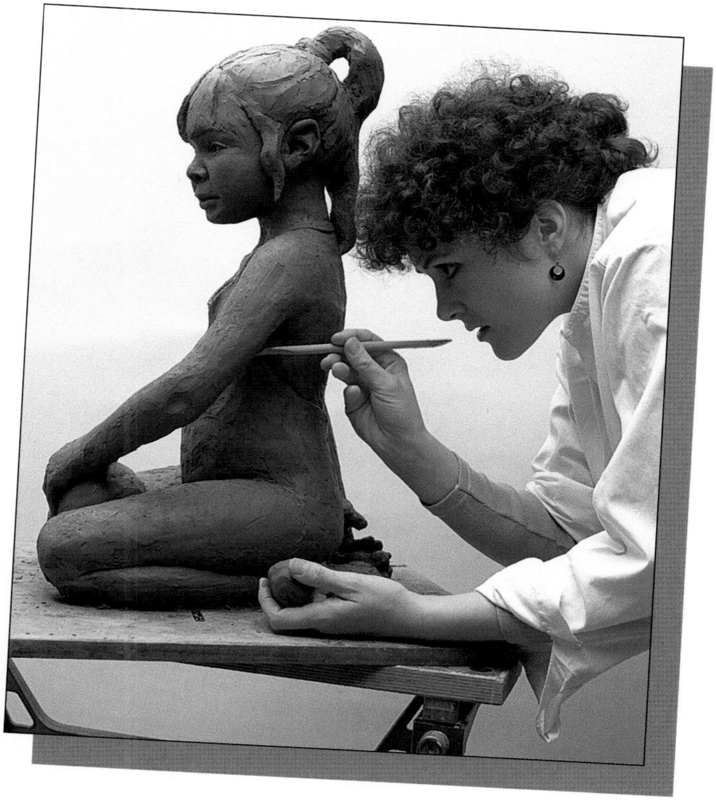

artist

At home

What are these tools used for?

Glossary

calculator *a machine that works out the answers to sums*
cutlery *tools that we use to eat with*
models *small versions of larger objects*
tool *an object that is held in the hand and used to do special jobs*

Index